BECOMING A
WOMAN *who* WALKS
WITH GOD

*To Carol,
my friend here
and in Heaven.
all my Heart,
Renee*

BECOMING A WOMAN *who* WALKS WITH GOD

A MONTH OF DEVOTIONALS *for* ABIDING IN CHRIST

CYNTHIA HEALD

NAVPRESS

Discipleship Inside Out™

NAVPRESS ●

Discipleship Inside Out™

NavPress is the publishing ministry of The Navigators, an international Christian organization and leader in personal spiritual development. NavPress is committed to helping people grow spiritually and enjoy lives of meaning and hope through personal and group resources that are biblically rooted, culturally relevant, and highly practical.

For a free catalog go to www.NavPress.com
or call 1.800.366.7788 in the United States or 1.800.839.4769 in Canada.

ISBN 978-1-57683-733-7

Cover Design: David Carlson Design
Cover Image: Masao Ota and Samba Photo/Photonica

Some of the anecdotal illustrations in this book are true to life and are included with the permission of the persons involved. All other illustrations are composites of real situations, and any resemblance to people living or dead is coincidental.

Unless otherwise identified, all Scripture quotations in this publication are taken from the *New American Standard Bible* (NASB), © The Lockman Foundation 1960, 1962, 1963, 1968, 1971, 1972, 1973, 1975, 1977. Other versions used include: the HOLY BIBLE: NEW INTERNATIONAL VERSION® (NIV®), Copyright © 1973, 1978, 1984 by International Bible Society, used by permission of Zondervan Publishing House, all rights reserved; *The New Testament in Modern English* (PH), J. B. Phillips Translator, © J. B. Phillips 1958, 1960, 1972, used by permission of Macmillan Publishing Company; the *Amplified New Testament* (AMP), © The Lockman Foundation 1954, 1958; *The Message: The New Testament in Contemporary Language* by Eugene H. Peterson, copyright ©1993, used by permission of NavPress Publishing Group; and the *Williams New Testament* (WMS) by Charles B. Williams, Copyright 1937, 1965, 1966, by Edith S. Williams, Moody Bible Institute of Chicago.

Printed in Canada

6 7 8 9 10 11 12 / 14 13 12 11 10

O God, I have tasted Thy goodness, and it has both satisfied me and made me thirsty for more. I am painfully conscious of my need of further grace. I am ashamed of my lack of desire. O God, the Triune God, I want to want Thee; I long to be filled with longing; I thirst to be made more thirsty still. Show me Thy glory, I pray Thee, so that I may know Thee indeed. Begin in mercy a new work of love within me. Say to my soul, "Rise up, my love, my fair one, and come away." Then give me grace to rise and follow Thee up from this misty lowland where I have wandered so long. In Jesus' name. Amen.

A. W. TOZER

Contents

Introduction

Deep in my heart is the constant prayer that I would be a woman who consistently walks with God. I know that apart from Christ, I can do nothing — at least, nothing that is selfless, truly satisfying, and eternal.

To walk with the Lord is to be with Him consistently, to go with Him where He wants me to go, to let Him set the pace, and to delight in His companionship above all others.

Essential to walking with God is maintaining unbroken communion with Him. This devotional book, designed to guide you through at least a month of quiet times, emphasizes the joy and the importance of abiding in Christ. My prayer is that these daily thoughts will encourage you to spend time with the Lord as they strengthen your heart to choose "the good part," the abiding that Mary of Bethany chose.

"By this we know that we are in Him: the one who says he abides in Him ought himself to walk in the same manner as He walked" (1 John 2:5-6).

God bless you richly as you abide in Him.

Love in Christ,

Cynthia Heald

1

The Security of Abiding

You must go on growing in me and I will grow in you.
For just as the branch cannot bear any fruit unless it shares
the life of the vine, so you can produce nothing
unless you go on growing in me.

John 15:4, PH

A small seashell sits on my desk. I found it years ago while looking for unusual shells. At first glance it seems quite ordinary, but close inspection reveals that it is actually two shells — a perfectly formed, smaller one completely encased by a larger one. The inner shell is delicate and fragile; the outer shell is solid and strong.

When I discovered this shell, I was captivated by how it pictures the concept of abiding in Christ. The small shell, because it is permanently fastened to the larger shell, is completely protected and secure. This is a wonderful visual image of abiding — staying, remaining, holding on to, continuing, dwelling, trusting.

I keep this shell as a reminder of the value of staying close to the Lord, but Jesus uses the illustration of a living vine and its branches to teach us about abiding. He tells us that He alone is the source of abundance and growth. We are the branches, and we must stay firmly connected to the Vine in order to mature. If a branch is broken off from the Vine, it will wither. If a branch is simply near the Vine without being attached to it, it will never flourish. Only as the branch remains united with the trunk can fruit be produced.

Abiding in Christ is deciding to let Christ be our Source, surrendering our life for His life, seeking His kingdom and His righteousness, trusting Him to provide all that we need. It is choosing each day to spend time with Him in His Word and in conversation with Him. To abide in Christ is to attach our delicate, fragile selves firmly and permanently into the Vine in order to receive His strength and security.

Jesus calls each of us to abide in Him. "Stay connected to Me," He invites us. As we choose to live in Him, He lives in us — and enables us to bear the lovely fruit of His character.

Have you ever thought what a wonderful privilege it is that everyone each day and each hour of the day has the liberty of asking God to meet him in the inner chamber and to hear what He has to say? We should imagine that every Christian would use such a privilege gladly and faithfully.

ANDREW MURRAY

REFLECT: In what areas of my life do I especially need the security of abiding in Christ?

Lord, I am just like the little shell. I am fragile and I need the protection and security that only You can give. I am humbled by your invitation to stay firmly connected to You. Thank you for Your presence in my life. May I faithfully abide in You. AMEN.

2

Choosing to Abide

Mary . . . was listening to the Lord's word, seated at His feet. But Martha was distracted with all her preparations; and she came up to Him, and said, "Lord, do You not care that my sister has left me to do all the serving alone? Then tell her to help me."

Luke 10:39-40

Have you ever felt neglected and unappreciated because nobody seemed to notice how hard you were working?

Picture Martha all alone in her kitchen, working as fast as she can to get a meal ready for guests. Imagine what she might have been thinking: *Isn't anyone aware of what I'm doing? Don't they realize how much work it takes to feed everyone? Why doesn't somebody think about me? It's bad enough that Mary isn't helping. Why doesn't Jesus notice how unfair this is?* The more she focuses on all she has to do, the more anxious she becomes.

The pressure builds until Martha just can't take it anymore. She strides into the sitting room and confronts Jesus, virtually reprimanding Him for not caring about her and her situation.

I love Martha for speaking openly and honestly with her Lord. And I love the Lord for always speaking the truth to all who come to Him.

Jesus receives Martha lovingly. He responds to her protest by encouraging her to realize that she can lay aside her tense preoccupation with tasks. He gives her the freedom to be concerned only with what is best, with what is eternal.

Jesus wants us to focus our lives on *being with* Him rather than on busying ourselves with *doing for* Him. He calls us to abide — to sit at His feet and listen to His words. Like Martha, we are called to change our center of attention from ourselves to Jesus.

This change enables us to offer service freely, not grudgingly. In fact, when our first priority is abiding, we cannot *help* but serve the Lord. Mary's heartfelt desire to be with Jesus later prompted her to serve Him by anointing Him with oil. Jesus praised her act and proclaimed that wherever the gospel was preached, it would be remembered (see John 12:1-3). Because Mary chose to sit at the feet of Jesus, when she did rise to serve Him, her ministry was profound.

In the midst of our "doing," may we stop to hear Jesus' counsel: "But the Lord answered and said to her, 'Martha, Martha, you are worried and bothered about so many things; but only a few things are necessary, really only one, for Mary has chosen the good part, which shall not be taken away from her'" (Luke 10:41-42).

"Mary has chosen what is better. . . . " He brings his point gently home: Fellowship with him is a matter of priorities. And a matter of choice. It's the better part of the meal life has to offer. It is, in fact, the main course.

KEN GIRE

REFLECT: What can I do today to choose the good part that Mary chose?

Lord, I don't want to go through life bothered and anxious. I don't want to eat haphazardly from Your table or give You the leftovers of my life. Sitting at Your feet is the good part of any day. Give me an undistracted heart so that I will abide in You. AMEN.

3

Abiding in the Word

I have not departed from the command of His lips;
I have treasured the words of His mouth
more than my necessary food.

Job 23:12

Eating is one of life's necessities — but it's a requirement that we can enjoy! I am always thankful when it's time to sit down and enjoy fellowship with others over a meal.

Aside from being pleasurable, eating is essential for strength and energy. Before a race, marathon runners carefully plan which foods to eat, so that they will have sufficient stamina for the long hours they will be running. When the Israelites were in the wilderness, God prepared food for them to gather daily so that they would have the endurance they needed for their prolonged journey.

God was concerned about the Israelites' physical requirements, but He was also teaching them to look to Him for all their needs — spiritual as well as physical. For just as our bodies need sustenance, so do our spirits need daily nourishment. Feeding our spirits is essential to our growth, strength, and ability to bear fruit. It is also something that can be very pleasurable.

The most enjoyable way I have found to nourish my spirit on a daily basis is to follow a reading program that takes me through the Scriptures each year. A plan (such as those recommended in certain study Bibles or specially arranged editions) keeps me on track — and encourages me to read Leviticus and Nahum! I like a schedule that combines Old Testament and New Testament portions each day. It takes only three or four chapters per day to read the whole Bible in a year, which averages about ten or fifteen minutes each day of listening to God in His Word.

"The Word of God will stand a thousand readings," it's been said, "and he who has gone over it most frequently is the surest of finding new wonders there." I love simply to read the Bible — without the pressure of answering questions, just to relax and enjoy the content of the Scriptures. This way of taking in the Word has a rich reward all its own.

"If you abide in My word," Jesus tells us, "then you are truly disciples of Mine" (John 8:31). A daily intake of the Scriptures is one of the surest ways of abiding in His Word. May we say with Jeremiah, "Thy words were found and I ate them, and Thy words became for me a joy and the delight of my heart . . . " (Jeremiah 15:16).

———

We must study His words, fairly devour His words, let them sink into our thought and into our heart, keep them in our memory, obey them constantly in our life, let them shape and mold our daily life and our every act. This is really the method of abiding in Christ. It is through His words that Jesus imparts Himself to us.

R. A. TORREY

REFLECT: When and where is the best opportunity for me to sit at the feet of Jesus each day, like Mary of Bethany, and listen to His Word?

Lord, I seem to find time to eat and do a lot of other necessary things throughout my day. Help me to set aside the time I need to do the most necessary thing to nurture my relationship with You. Give me a hunger and thirst for righteousness and the discipline to strengthen my spirit each day so that I can "run the race" for Your glory. AMEN.

4

Bearing Fruit

I am the vine, you are the branches; he who abides in Me,
and I in him, he bears much fruit;
for apart from Me you can do nothing.

John 15:5

One of the most challenging passages in the Scriptures, and a personal favorite of mine, is John 15. Jesus is gathered with His disciples in what will be their final evening together. He knows that the time for fulfilling His mission is near, and so these last few hours with His disciples are precious. He wants to impart to them His very heart; He wants to leave them with truth that they will never forget.

The Scriptures give us the privilege of listening in on this intimate encounter. As I read this passage, I like to imagine how it would feel to be one of the disciples in the Upper Room with Jesus. As I listen to Him speak, I respond in my heart to His teaching.

"I am the Vine, and you are the branches."

—Lord, how easy it is for me to confuse our relationship! I tend to act as if I am the vine. I try to live life in my own strength instead of depending on You for guidance, nourishment, and grace. No wonder the fruit in my life seems to dry up and disappear.

"Your responsibility is to abide in Me and to let Me abide in you."

—Jesus, You are asking me to take time to stay in Your presence, to allow You to live continuously in me. Sometimes this seems very hard to do. Yet it is as simple as consistently sitting at Your feet with a desire to obey.

"The key to fruitbearing is to stay connected to the Vine."

—Lord, You have said that apart from You I can do nothing. The only way to be fruitful, to become like You, is to stay united to You. I don't want to live a fruitless life, yet that's what happens when I try to bear fruit with my own efforts. Perhaps this is why I struggle so often to live the Christian life. Instead of striving and straining, my great need is just to be still and abide.

"You can do many things without depending on Me, but one thing you cannot do is bear fruit."

—Lord, You say that whoever abides in You will bear *much* fruit. This is what I desire. To do this I know that I must give up my independence. I surrender myself to Your power to transform me according to Your likeness. I yield my life to bear the priceless fruit that is the product of abiding.

This imaginative encounter is, of course, my own rendering. But we know that the last words of Jesus to His disciples before His death and resurrection are also our Lord's words to each of us. They give us the key to fruitfulness in the life of faith: *abide in Christ*.

That's what life in Christ is all about — abiding.
It is not the fruit-producing that matters, it is the abiding.
The producing comes from the vine; the branches are only
the fruit bearers. To be an abiding branch is to be a faithful
branch. The fruit will come. And the fruit that is borne,
whether it be large fruit or small, abundant or not so
abundant, is his doing. Our role is to be attached to
the vine, to fit into our place — to abide.

ROGER C. PALMS

REFLECT: What hinders me from bearing *much* fruit in
my life?

Lord, please help me to understand that I don't need to strive and
strain in my walk with You. You are the Vine; I am the branch.
You want me to rest in You, to share Your life, to allow You to
produce fruit in my life. I want to be like You, and I want to bear
"much" fruit of abiding. AMEN.

5

One Day at a Time

Don't worry at all then about tomorrow.
Tomorrow can take care if itself! . . .

Matthew 6:34, PH

I sat down at my desk recently to try to make sense out of my schedule. It turned out to be a frustrating task. In the midst of feeling burdened by a heavy load of future responsibilities and pressed down by all the demands of life, I sensed the Lord telling me, "Take one day at a time."

As I listen to friends share their difficulties and anxieties, I find myself saying, "Keep fixing your eyes on Jesus, and just take one day at a time." It sounds simple. Yet there is great relief in recognizing afresh that our lives are in the Lord's hands.

We need to live *today* as much as we can to the glory of God. Let us spend time with the Lord *today*, so we can firmly grasp His will. Let us make the best use of our time *today*, and cast our care for tomorrow on Him. As the *Phillips* translation of Matthew 6:34 reads, "One day's trouble is enough for one day."

The Lord invites us to release our burdens into His

care. Our heavenly Father knows what we need. How freeing it is to let go of our anxiety about the "what-ifs" of our lives and focus instead on seeking His kingdom and His righteousness.

"Live life, then, with a due sense of responsibility, not as men who do not know the meaning of life but as those who do. Make the best use of your time, despite all the evils of these days. Don't be vague, but firmly grasp what you know to be the will of the Lord" (Ephesians 5:15-17, PH).

We must try to take life moment by moment.
The actual present is usually pretty tolerable
I think, if only we refrain from adding to its burden
that of the past and the future.

C. S. LEWIS

REFLECT: Where in my life do I especially need the freedom to live one day at a time?

Lord, You make it clear that we are not to worry about tomorrow. Thank You for such definite instruction in how to live. Teach me to lay aside anxiety and to focus on today's needs and opportunities. I know that my time with You gives me wisdom and sensitivity to meet each day. So let me live today in Your strength, for Your glory. AMEN.

6

Flying First Class

Peace I leave with you;
My peace I give to you;
not as the world gives, do I give to you.
Let not your heart be troubled,
nor let it be fearful.

John 14:27

As I arrived at the airport for a cross-country trip, I received a pleasant surprise. Due to an abundance of frequent-flier miles, I had been granted a first-class upgrade on my flight.

I boarded the plane ahead of the crowd and was greeted by name. I settled into a wide and comfortable seat, in close proximity to the pilot. The food was excellent, and the service I received was graciously given.

The trip was not entirely smooth, however. Approximately halfway through the flight we encountered some rough weather. As I reflected on my situation, I realized that although being seated in first class did not exempt me from experiencing turbulence, it made it somehow easier to endure.

Perhaps flying in first class provides a glimpse of the benefits of abiding. When we choose to abide in Christ, it doesn't mean that we will escape hardship. However, as we stay close to Him, we will experience the inner calm of His indwelling presence. Instead of being overwhelmed with the turbulence of life, we will experience His grace, His comfort, His intimacy, and His peace.

Traveling in first class is the most comfortable way to fly. Abiding in Christ is the most privileged way to live.

All the day long there is the pressure of life,
and perhaps some inner strain to the spirit known only to God.
But all the day long, too, there is the lovingkindness of God.
And so all the day long the peace that passes
all understanding. . . . The peace of Jesus stood every sort
of test, every strain, and it never broke. It is this,
His very own peace, which He says I give.

AMY CARMICHAEL

REFLECT: What are some ways in which I have experienced the peace of abiding in Jesus?

Calm in the midst of trials — that's what I need, Lord. Again, I am reminded that it is in abiding that I experience Your peace. Abiding frees me to enjoy Your goodness and enables me to receive Your very best. Thank you for the abundant blessing of abiding. AMEN.

7

"My" God Cares

"I love Thee, O LORD, my strength."
The LORD is my rock and my fortress and my deliverer,
My God, my rock, in whom I take refuge;
My shield and the horn of my salvation, my stronghold.

Psalm 18:1-2

Have you ever noticed how many times the word *my* is used in Psalm 18?

The dictionary defines *my* as "belonging or pertaining to me." The psalmist invites each of us to say with him, "God is mine!" His song of praise is filled with descriptions of the many ways in which God's personal care surrounds him.

He is *my* strength — "For by Thee I can run upon a troop; and by my God I can leap over a wall" (verse 29).

He is *my* rock — "Thou dost enlarge my steps under me; and my feet have not slipped" (verse 36).

He is *my* fortress and stronghold — "I call upon the LORD, who is worthy to be praised, and I am saved from my enemies" (verse 3).

He is *my* deliverer — "He brought me forth also into a broad place; He rescued me, because He delighted in me" (verse 19).

He is *my* shield — "He is a shield to all who take

refuge in Him" (verse 30).

God's care for us is so personal, Jesus tells us, that He knows the very number of hairs we have on our head (even the gray ones!). His thoughts about us outnumber the grains of sand on all the beaches of the world. He longs to be our strength in weakness, our light in darkness, our shelter in the storms of life, our deliverer in the midst of temptation, and our shield from anything that would threaten to destroy us.

May we respond with David, "Therefore I will give thanks to Thee among the nations, O LORD, and I will sing praises to Thy name" (verse 49).

For there is that in God which is suited to all the exigencies and occasions of his people that trust in him. "He is my rock, and strength, and fortress"; that is, "I have found him so in the greatest dangers and difficulties. I have chosen him to be so, disclaiming all others, and depending upon him alone to protect me." Those that truly love God may thus triumph in him as theirs, and may with confidence call upon him.

MATTHEW HENRY

REFLECT: Do I call upon the Lord as *my* God?

Lord, how can I thank You for all You are to me? You care for me, You know me, You love me. Forgive me for wanting anyone or anything else to be my protection or security. You are my *God, and You are enough.* AMEN.

8

God with Us

Therefore the Lord Himself will give you a sign:
Behold, a virgin will be with child and bear a son,
and she will call His name Immanuel.

Isaiah 7:14

While praying recently, I poured out to the Lord my concern about a future commitment. As I sat before Him, I sensed His presence and His words in my heart: *Cynthia, I am with you. Do not be anxious. I will continue to be with you.*

So often when we are discouraged or afraid, we lose sight of the reality of God's presence with us. Circumstances overwhelm us and make us wonder whether God is really with us and whether He is interested in the details of our lives.

We need never doubt the truth of God's presence with us. Jesus Christ is *Immanuel*—a name that literally means "God with us." Christ's life, death, and resurrection are the supreme evidence that God will go to any lengths — even paying the ultimate cost of His only Son — to dwell among His people.

God is truly with us . . .
Wherever we are.

Whenever we feel abandoned or alone.

Whatever circumstances we are going through. It is our privilege to be in relationship with God for eternity. This is why He came to earth, and this is why He died. May our lives be filled with *Immanuel*.

[For] those times when you yearn for my fellowship and stand at the door and knock, grant me a special sensitivity to the sound of that knock so I may be quick to my feet. Keep me from letting you stand out in the cold or from ever sending you away to some stable. May my heart be warm and inviting, so that when you do knock, a worthy place will always be waiting.

KEN GIRE

REFLECT: What is one significant way that God has used to awaken me to the reality of His abiding presence?

Lord, it overwhelms me that You never leave me or forsake me. You want to abide in me! Thank You for the reminder that I am never alone — for You are my Immanuel. AMEN.

9

Following in His Presence

Then [Moses] said to Him,
"If Thy presence does not go with us,
do not lead us up from here."

Exodus 33:15

When God led the Israelites through the wilderness between Egypt and the Promised Land, He gave them signs of His presence with them — a cloud by day, a pillar of fire by night. He provided manna, water, and meat in response to their complaints. But it seemed that even miraculous signs were never enough to quiet their restless doubt — "Is the Lord among us or not?"

When Moses disappeared into a cloud on Mount Sinai for weeks on end, the people's doubt hardened into rebellion. No longer content to follow in God's presence, they made themselves an idol out of jewelry and then proclaimed it a god.

Because of Israel's sin, God told Moses that in place of His presence He would send a guardian angel to accompany them into the Promised Land. Moses immediately began to pray earnestly for the Lord's presence in their midst. "If You don't go with us, please don't make us go at all," he cried out. "We'll be just like all the other tribes on the face of the earth. How will anyone know we belong to You?"

Moses knew, in a very real sense, that he could do nothing without God. Without the attendance and guidance of God Himself, the Israelites could not carry out God's will.

How often do we take the time to be assured of God's leadership, direction, and presence as we go on our way? His Spirit indwells us. Yet we tend to run off in our own direction, presuming that the way we are going is His will.

Too often I mistakenly think that I don't have time to wait for the Lord's guidance! What a contrast to the way Moses lived — if the Lord was not going to lead him all the way, then he was not moving.

How easy it is to become restless and distracted amid the anxieties and frustrations of our days. How easy it is to turn away from following God and rely on our own wisdom or be swayed by others' ideas. Yet our failure to rely on God's guidance leaves us more lost in the wilderness than ever before. Each day of our lives, in each moment of our day, let us delight in waiting for God's presence to lead us.

———

He who begins, finishes. He who leads us on,
follows behind to deal in love with our poor attempts. . . .
He gathers up the things that we have dropped — our fallen
resolutions, our mistakes. . . . He makes His blessed
pardon to flow over our sins till they are utterly washed
away. And He turns to fight the Enemy, who would
pursue after us, to destroy us from behind.

AMY CARMICHAEL

REFLECT: This day, how can I live by abiding in God's presence instead of going my own way?

Lord, You are gracious, patient, and committed to me. May I develop the same sensitivity as Moses, who knew that any step without You would ultimately end in futility. Help me to long for Your presence and to wait patiently for Your leading. AMEN.

10

The Grace of Patience

The fruit of the Spirit is love, joy, peace, patience. . . .
Galatians 5:22

Years ago when our children were small, we all memorized Galatians 5:22-23, which describes the fruit of abiding in the Spirit. To make it fun, we numbered each fruit in consecutive order: "love" was one ... "patience" was four ... "gentleness" was eight ... and so forth.

In our family interactions, we often found ourselves calling out numbers to each other. I remember many times as I was driving somewhere in a hurry, my children would say, "Mom — number four!" Actually, this was the number we announced most often in our family. Perhaps for many of us, patience is one of the more difficult fruits to bear!

My idea of developing patience is to spend time with the Lord reading His Word and praying ... then rise up and just be patient! I tend to forget that as I abide in the Vine, the Vinedresser *prunes* my branch to bear more fruit. Pruning means to reduce eliminating superfluous matter; to cut off or cut back parts of a plant for better shape or more fruitful growth. It is this pruning that produces patience.

Having three children in three years was a great pruning experience in my life. It was God's creative way of putting me in a situation where I had to learn patience — indeed, all of the fruits of the Spirit — in a practical, experiential way. Having a busy husband and eventually a fourth child was a major way of reducing the nonessential parts of my life and teaching me to concentrate on what was most important. As I look back now I can hear Him saying to me, "Cynthia, that was for number four!"

God wants to cut back the nonessentials in our lives so that we will be more able to draw our life from one source — the Vine. This process can be painful, but it is always for our good. As we yield to God's loving desire to snip or sever the extraneous twigs and branches in our lives, we will learn endurance and trust. Increasingly, this develops within us a calm and patient spirit — the evidence of *His* fruit in our lives.

———

*[The] grace of patience — which is either the meek
endurance of ill because it is of God, or the calm waiting
for promised good till His time to dispense it comes — [is]
the full persuasion that such trials are divinely appointed,
are the needed discipline of God's children, are but
for a definite period, and are not sent without
abundant promises of "songs in the night."*

ROBERT JAMIESON, ET AL.

———

REFLECT: What is my deepest need for cultivating patience at this time in my life?

Lord, I need Your grace to endure the pruning process through which You produce patience, and all the other fruit of the Spirit, in me. Keep me close as I abide in You. Help me to rejoice in the experiences that are necessary to shape me into becoming more like You. AMEN.

11

Rest and Wait

*Rest in the LORD
and wait patiently for Him. . . .*
Psalm 37:7

I find it very difficult to wait. Red lights and long lines readily provoke my impatient spirit. So while I was reading in Psalm 37, I stopped at verse 7 and asked myself, *Do I really rest and wait?* As Charles Spurgeon comments, "This requires much grace to carry out!"

To *rest* can be translated to "be silent" or to "hold still." To *wait* means to "stay or rest in expectation or patience." Jerome, an early church scholar, declared that it is easier to carry out even a *difficult* command to action than it is to obey this "command to inaction."

My problem (and it was Martha's) is that I like to be *doing.* Sitting still is hard for me. How I need to remember that my timing may not be God's timing. He alone knows when and what will best accomplish His purposes.

J. Oswald Sanders tells the story of how a friend of the distinguished preacher Phillips Brooks stopped by to see him one day and found Brooks pacing up and down the room in great agitation.

"What's the matter, Phillips?" asked the friend.

"Matter enough," came the reply. "I am in a hurry and God is not."

Our God is patient and long-suffering. He is never in a hurry, and He is seldom on our time schedule! Yet He is our Father, who is continually working all things together for our good. And so He tells us to *rest*—to be calm and peaceful; and to *wait*—to anticipate, to count upon, to watch for Him. A good way to respond to the complexities of life!

It is our duty and our privilege to wait upon the Lord in service, in worship, in expectancy, in trust all the days of our life. Our faith will be a tried faith, and if it be of the true kind, it will bear continued trial without yielding. We shall not grow weary of waiting upon God if we remember how long and how graciously He once waited for us.

CHARLES SPURGEON

REFLECT: Is there a problem or concern that I would like to turn over to God's keeping this day?

Lord, You know what is best for my life. Thank You for telling me so clearly that I need to rest and wait. I'm not sure that I truly know how to do that, but I want to live the way that You have shown me. And I know that I can do that as I abide in You. AMEN.

12

Responding to Painful Circumstances

*Through Him then, let us continually offer up
a sacrifice of praise to God, that is,
the fruit of lips that give thanks to His name.*

Hebrews 13:15

———————◈———————

While one of my children was going through a very hurtful situation, I found it difficult to give thanks or to praise God in this circumstance. In light of this experience I am struck by the exhortation in Hebrews 13:15 — we are asked to make a *sacrifice* of praise to God.

To sacrifice means to surrender, relinquish, or yield. When we make a sacrifice, we are offering up a gift. It encourages me to know that my praise is often a sacrifice — a gift to God and a release for me.

I think of the sacrifice Abraham was asked to make when God tested him by requesting that he surrender his only son, Isaac, as a burnt offering. I am amazed when I read in the Scriptures that after God's request, "Abraham rose early in the morning" (Genesis 22:3). All sacrifice, whether great or small, entails obedience. Abraham's obedience was founded upon trust in God.

He was willing to relinquish his son because he knew that God would provide whatever was necessary to keep His promise to multiply Abraham's descendants through Isaac — if necessary, even by raising Isaac from the dead.

Abraham's prompt response to God is echoed in Job's reaction upon learning of the loss of his entire estate and all his children. His immediate response was to begin mourning by falling to the ground and worshiping God: "The LORD gave and the LORD has taken away. Blessed be the name of the LORD," he cried (Job 1:21). This painful sacrifice of praise was rooted in Job's unconditional trust in the character of God. This trust bore fruit in faith and obedience instead of doubt and rebellion.

Praise, particularly in difficult circumstances, arises from a desire to obey God and to trust His ways. Perhaps the Lord wants us to offer praise because in this "sacrifice" we are released from the bondage of anxiety and freed to see His hand working all things together for good. We are able to offer "the fruit of lips" that give thanks in all things — a fruit that is cultivated only through abiding in Christ.

Thanksgiving gives effect to prayer and frees us from anxious carefulness by making all God's dealings a matter for praise, not merely for resignation, much less murmuring. Peace is the companion of thanksgiving.

ROBERT JAMIESON, ET AL.

REFLECT: What tends to hinder me from praising God in painful circumstances?

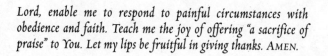

Lord, enable me to respond to painful circumstances with obedience and faith. Teach me the joy of offering "a sacrifice of praise" to You. Let my lips be fruitful in giving thanks. AMEN.

13

Protection from Discouragement

The LORD himself goes before you and will be with you;
he will never leave you nor forsake you.
Do not be afraid; do not be discouraged.

Deuteronomy 31:8, NIV

───────⟨⟩───────

The words of great encouragement in Deuteronomy
31:8 were spoken by Moses to Joshua as the
Israelites were on the verge of crossing the Jordan River
into the Promised Land. As Moses' successor, Joshua was
to lead them. What an incredible task! Taking a whole
nation into an unconquered land, without Moses, must
have seemed an overwhelming assignment. But the Lord
knew the exact words Joshua would need to cling to in
the days and years ahead.

When I was a little girl, whenever there was a new
challenge or an unfamiliar path I would say to my friend,
"You go first." I always felt reassured when someone else
took the lead.

Sometimes, when we look at the rivers in our lives
that we must cross, we become disheartened. When we
listen to the news, it seems that evil is surpassing good.
But the Lord knows we need hope to face the journey
ahead, so we can take heart from His words to Joshua.

"The LORD himself goes before you and will be with you." How great our security and confidence when we know that the Lord Himself is leading us — and that He will stay with us.

"He will never leave you nor forsake you." Our God will not abandon us. The rivers may be deep or difficult to cross, but they will not overwhelm us.

"Do not be afraid; do not be discouraged." This is a command! But it is given in the same breath as the promise of His steadfast presence and protection.

Our Lord knows that the struggles and uncertainties of life can leave us feeling dismayed and anxious. He offers us the assurance of His ultimate victory over all that would defeat us: "In the world you have tribulation, but take courage; I have overcome the world" (John 16:33).

Were our God a novice in the great art of governing the world,
and of the church in the bosom thereof; had he to this day
never given any proof of his infinite wisdom, power,
and goodness, in turning about the most terrible accidents
to the welfare and joy of his saints; we might indeed
be amazed whenever we feel ourselves sinking in
the dangers wherein the practices of our enemies
oft do plunge us over head and ears; but the Lord
having given in times past so many documents
of his uncontroverted skill and most certain will
to bring about all human affairs, as to his own glory,
so to the real good of all that love him, it would be
in us an impious and inexcusable uncharitableness
to suspect the end of any work which he hath begun.

ROBERT BAYLIE

REFLECT: How can I be encouraged this day by the truth that the Lord "goes before me" to accomplish His purposes in my life?

Lord, thank You for Your trustworthiness, Your protection, Your unfailing presence. Strengthen me to realize that I need not live my life in fear or discouragement, for You are my Cod, and You are always with me. AMEN.

14
The Power of Perseverance

Moreover — let us also be full of joy now!
Let us exult and triumph in our troubles and rejoice
in our sufferings knowing that pressure and affliction
and hardship produce patient and unswerving endurance.

Romans 5:3, AMP

After visiting with a close friend and listening to her ongoing heartaches, I felt that the only thing I could do was encourage her to persevere — to face her pressures and trials with a steadfast commitment to do right and to maintain a godly life.

In the Greek, perseverance means "to patiently endure." Our English definition means "to persist or remain constant to a purpose, idea, or task in the face of obstacles."

After encouraging us to persevere, Paul goes on in Romans 5 to illuminate the fruit of our perseverance: "And endurance (fortitude) develops maturity of character — that is, approved faith and tried integrity. And character (of this sort) produces (the habit of) joyful and confident hope of eternal salvation. Such hope never disappoints or deludes or shames us, for God's love has been poured out in our hearts through the Holy Spirit who has been given to us" (verses 4-5, AMP).

Persevering and *enduring* are not exactly cheerful words! Yet they are powerful and necessary in our lives. No matter who we are, who we know, or what our status is in life, we all go through trials. How encouraging to know that persevering through these experiences produces a beautiful result: our character matures, and so does our ability to place our hope in God and to experience God's love.

It is much easier to persevere when we remain closely connected to our source of strength and grace. Abiding in Christ enables us to endure, even rejoice in, the hardship that God allows in our lives.

This persevering is a hard word! Taking up the cross daily, praying always, watching night and day and never laying aside our armour to indulge ourselves, sends many sorrowful away from Christ. Yet this is your calling: to make the Christian faith your daily work, without any vacation from one end of the year to the other.

WILLIAM GURNALL

REFLECT: In what areas of my life is God calling me to persevere in the face of struggle or heartache?

Lord, I confess that I want the love, joy, and peace that come from abiding, but I tend to back away from trouble and suffering. Teach me what it means to persevere. Teach me to value the affliction in my life. Remind me that hardship produces patient and unswerving endurance. AMEN.

15

Joy in Trials

You must consider it the purest joy, my brothers,
when you are involved in various trials.

James 1:2, WMS

I have always found it very hard to consider it "pure joy" when I am encountering various trials. During a period in which I was experiencing many different tests in my life, I began meditating on James 1:2-4.

I soon realized that my attitude toward experiencing trials determines whether or not I truly believe that it is a joy to go through them. If I consider them unwelcome burdens, I will chafe at them in resentment — and miss any opportunity to experience the joy that God offers in the midst of them.

Essentially, trials should make us more dependent upon the Lord by helping us realize that we cannot live life in our own strength. As we depend upon and draw strength from God, we grow in endurance — the ability to continue in the same state without perishing; to suffer without resistance or compromise; to bear without opposition or sinking under pressure.

The joy of encountering hardship springs from the

knowledge that God is at work in our lives to make us more like Him. It is our choice to trust God with our lives so that steadfastness under pressure enables us to mature in Christ, fully prepared to be useful to the Lord. As *The Message* renders James 1:4, "Don't try to get out of anything prematurely. Let it do its work so you become mature and well-developed, not deficient in any way." If we want to bear much fruit, then we will "consider it the purest joy when we are involved in various trials." Let us determine to abide faithfully through difficulties as we allow them to shape us into becoming more like Jesus Christ.

———

Wrap your weary souls in this promise: There is a place of rest reserved for the people of God. You do not beat the air, but wrestle to win heaven and a permanent crown. Here on earth we overcome to fight again. One temptation may be conquered, but the war remains. When death comes, however, God strikes the final blow. We know peace is sweet after war, pleasure after pain. But what tongue can express the joy that will flood the creature at the first sight of God and his eternal home? If we knew more of that future blissful state, we would worry less about our present conflict.

WILLIAM GURNALL

———

REFLECT: What do I need to change in my life in order to begin to experience joy in the midst of trials?

———

Lord, it is so easy for me to resent hardship as an unwelcome interruption of my plans and desires. Melt my resistance. Open my heart to the joy of yielding to Your work in my life, because I know that Your ways are best. AMEN.

16

Unconditional Trust

Trust in the LORD with all your heart,
And do not lean on your own understanding.
In all your ways acknowledge Him,
And He will make your paths straight.

Proverbs 3:5-6

The wise counsel of Proverbs 3:5-6 has been in my heart for over twenty-five years. Although it has become an old friend, its encouragement continues to be fresh and new in my life.

During a recent struggle, it seemed that the Lord was saying to me, "Do you trust Me?"

My response was, "Yes, Lord, I trust You. But can't You rephrase the question, 'Do you trust Me to work everything out so that you are happy?' I think I could *really* trust You then."

But the Lord was steadfast: the issue was my *unconditional* trust. No strings attached, no negotiating, no promises.

In a deeper way, I began to understand what it means to trust God with *all* my heart. There is no room for bargaining for what I think is best — only implicit confidence and patience in His plan.

The Scriptures do not guarantee that "all will be

well" according to our human perspective. They do, however, promise that God will work all things for our good. As we learn to trust Him "no matter what," He develops within us a deeply rooted confidence in Him. This confidence enables us to lean on *His* understanding and *His* ways of working in our lives.

I like the *Amplified* version of Proverbs 3:5-6: "Lean on, trust and be confident in the Lord with all your heart and mind, and do not rely on your own insight or understanding. In all your ways know, recognize and acknowledge Him, and He will direct and make straight and plain your paths."

Is God asking you to trust Him unconditionally? If so, then be encouraged: He is developing within you a confidence that will enable you to draw more deeply from life in the Vine.

———

All the way my Savior leads me —
What have I to ask beside?
Can I doubt His tender mercy,
Who through life has been my guide?
Heavenly peace, divinest comfort,
Here by faith in Him to dwell!
For I know, whate'er befall me,
Jesus doeth all things well.

FANNY J. CROSBY

———

REFLECT: What are the challenges in my life that especially call for wholehearted trust, no matter what?

Lord, You are very gracious. You give a good return for total trust — You grant me freedom from trying to figure everything out and assurance that I'm on the right path. Teach me to lean on, trust, and be confident in You with all my heart. AMEN.

17

Suffering and Glory

*For I consider that the sufferings of this present time
are not worthy to be compared with the glory
that is to be revealed to us.*

Romans 8:18

There was a bittersweet song many years ago that posed the question, "Is this all there is?" For those who do not have a personal relationship with the living God through His Son, Jesus Christ, that is a very valid question. Those without Christ have no authentic hope. All they can cling to is this present, earthly life.

The good news is that once we have experienced new life in Christ, we are born again to eternal life. We gain a true home in heaven and a brand-new perspective on life. Our life on earth is but a fleeting moment in comparison to spending eternity with the Lord.

Despite the glorious hope of what is to come, however, we still struggle with the here-and-now. Believers undergo the same suffering that afflicts all humanity. There are times when the hardships become so intense that we are tempted to ask, "Lord, is this all there is to the Christian life?"

We find a resting place for this question in Paul's wise counsel in 2 Corinthians 4:17-18. I like J. B. Phillips' translation: "These little troubles (which are really so transitory) are winning for us a permanent, glorious and solid reward out of all proportion to our pain. For we are looking all the time not at the visible things but at the invisible. The visible things are transitory: it is the invisible things that are really permanent."

How good it is to be reminded that "this present time" is not all there is. Maintaining an eternal perspective is key to responding to the challenges we face now. Heaven is our permanent home, and it is truly going to be glorious! The hymn "Amazing Grace" paints a lovely picture of what it will be like: "When we've been there ten thousand years, bright shining as the sun, we've no less days to sing God's praise than when we'd first begun."

O God, quicken to life every power within me, that I may lay hold on eternal things. Open my eyes that I may see; give me acute spiritual perception; enable me to taste Thee and know that Thou art good. Make heaven more real to me than any earthly thing has ever been.

A. W. TOZER

REFLECT: How different is my perspective on present sufferings when I view them in light of the promise of coming glory?

Lord, thank You for the reminder to keep an eternal perspective. Help me to focus on what is of lasting worth so that I do not become distracted by what is merely of passing value. Your Word says, "If we hope for what we do not see, with perseverance we wait eagerly for it." Teach me to live my life in the light of eternity. AMEN.

18

The Faithfulness of God

*My soul, wait in silence for God only, For my hope is from
Him. He only is my rock and my salvation, My stronghold;
I shall not be shaken. On God my salvation and my glory
rest; The rock of my strength, my refuge is in God.*

Psalm 62:5-7

O ne evening my husband, Jack, and I were attending
a banquet when a young man recognized Jack and
came over to sit down next to him. Then two other couples who knew each other, but not us, joined our table.
The seating left an empty chair next to me. We all introduced ourselves, visited briefly, and then dinner began.

Once the food was served, everyone at our table
began conversing with each other — except me. I realized that the rest of the meal would most likely continue
in this way, and I began to feel isolated and alone. I even
felt as if people at nearby tables must be whispering
about how sad it was that Cynthia was such a pitiful case
that no one wanted to sit next to her or talk to her!

As I was busy feeling sorry for myself, the Lord's
gentle voice spoke to my heart: *Cynthia, is it true that no one
is noticing you?*

I replied, *Oh, Lord, I know that You love me and that You
are with me now, but look at all these other people — they're having*

a good time and I'm all by myself!

Then came the question, *Cynthia, isn't My love enough?*

I thought of the words of Psalm 62: "He only is my rock and my salvation, My stronghold; I shall not be shaken." *Yes, Lord,* I answered, *Your love is enough. You only are my salvation, my stronghold, the rock of my strength, my refuge. In You, I am complete and lack for nothing. You are always enough.*

Seating arrangements at a dinner table may seem like a minor episode. Yet the clutch of insecurity I felt was very real. Essentially, it was the fear of abandonment. My experience at that banquet became a precious reminder to me of how God is faithful to abide with us in every moment of our lives — from the "little" events to the big ones. Let us respond gladly to the psalmist's invitation: "Trust in Him at all times, O people; pour out your heart before Him; God is a refuge for us" (62:8).

Alone, and without other help, God is the foundation and completion of my safety. We cannot too often hear the toll of that great bell, only; let it ring the death-knell of all carnal reliances, and lead us to cast ourselves on the arm of God . . . I am secure, because he is faithful.

CHARLES SPURGEON

REFLECT: In what areas of life do I desire to take refuge in the faithfulness of God?

Lord, You are faithful; You never leave me nor forsake me. Forgive me when I forget Your loving faithfulness to me. Teach me to wait for You, to hope in You, and to depend on You alone for my security. AMEN.

19

Strength for the Weary

*Do you not know? Have you not heard? The Everlasting God, the L*ORD*, the Creator of the ends of the earth Does not become weary or tired. His understanding is inscrutable. He gives strength to the weary, And to him who lacks might He increases power.*

Isaiah 40:28-29

O ften the highlight of my day is when I go to bed at night! I am weary and ready to rest. Most of the time this is a physical exhaustion, and I simply need a good night's sleep. I'm reminded of the verse, "For He gives to His beloved even in his sleep" (Psalm 127:2). Physical rest supplies physical strength.

But where do we go for rest when we are emotionally and spiritually weary? Isaiah brings us the good news ("Have you not heard?") — our eternal God abounds in strength and understanding, and He gives His strength and power to the faint. "For I satisfy the weary ones and refresh everyone who languishes," God proclaims in Jeremiah 31:25.

What an encouragement to know that this is God's desire. Yet how do we receive His refreshment? Isaiah continues, "But those who *wait* for the Lord (who expect, look for, and hope in Him) shall change and renew their strength and power. . ." (Isaiah 40:31, AMP). Here is the key to spiritual strength: to be still, fixing our eyes on the Lord. Another way of saying this is simply *to rest and abide*.

When I am in dire need of spiritual and emotional strengthening, I cry out to the Lord, "What am I to do?" His answer is always the same: "Come to Me, all you who labor and are heavy-laden and over burdened, and I will cause you to rest — I will ease and relieve and refresh your souls" (Matthew 11:28, AMP).

Many a time he gives power to the faint, to those that are ready to faint away; and to those that have no might he not only gives, but increases strength, as there is more and more occasion for it. . . . To those who are sensible of their weakness, and ready to acknowledge they have no might, God does in a special manner increase strength; for, when we are weak in ourselves, then we are strong in the Lord.

MATTHEW HENRY

REFLECT: Where do I especially need to acknowledge my own weakness in order to draw strength from the Lord?

Lord, I know that when I am tired, I need to rest. Yet when I need strength for my soul, why is it so hard for me to come to You and wait before You? Thank You that You give strength to the weary. Help me to remember that You alone can renew my spirit. AMEN.

20

The Potter and the Clay

. . . O LORD, Thou art our Father,
We are the clay, and Thou our potter;
And all of us are the work of Thy hand.

Isaiah 64:8

———————————

The older I get, the more I realize that I'm not going to be permitted to live my life on my own terms! I'm beginning to understand that I can't control other people or my circumstances, and that God, my heavenly Father, is in the continual process of using all things to mold my life.

One summer I had plans to fly to Louisville and meet my mother there for a convention. She was arriving from Houston and I was flying in from Tucson, and we had agreed to meet in the baggage claim area. But when I arrived at the airport I learned that my Tucson-to-Phoenix flight was delayed, which meant that I would miss my connecting flight to Louisville and arrive several hours later than I had been scheduled. I began to worry about getting word to my mom. How would she get transportation to the hotel without me? I pictured her waiting for me in the bustling baggage claim area, alone and bewildered.

To my surprise, the Tucson gate agent whisked a few of us away to another airline, and within minutes we were airborne. The timing was very tight, but it looked like I just might make it. Then I realized that once we landed in Phoenix, we would have to transfer to another terminal to make our connection. There was no way we could make that flight. *Lord, I can't believe this is happening!* I protested. *This is a totally frustrating situation!*

But there was a second surprise waiting for me. In Phoenix, an agent greeted us out on the tarmac to escort us to our connecting flight, which was being held just for us. As we stepped out of the airplane, he pointed out that our luggage was accompanying us, too. Once again, within minutes we were on our way, and I was able to meet my mom right on time.

This was not how I had designed my day, but it was God's plan. I was reminded that He is the potter, and I am the clay. He was creating something in me through this experience. By the end of the trip my trust was strengthened in His sovereign power to go before me and to be with me. My clay was a little freer of anxiety, for I realized that worry accomplishes nothing. My life was reshaped with praise, for I knew my God was for me. How thankful I am that He is our Potter.

Oh, be generous in your self-surrender! Meet His measureless devotion for you with a measureless devotion to Him. Be glad and eager to throw yourself unreservedly into His loving arms, and to hand over the reins of government to Him. Whatever there is of you, let Him have it all.

HANNAH WHITALL SMITH

REFLECT: At what times do I find it most difficult to place myself without reservation in the Potter's hands?

Lord, Your ways are not my ways. Sometimes they are surprising, but they are always good and for my benefit. Teach me to let go of my life and place it in Your hands. Keep molding and shaping me in Your image and for Your glory. AMEN.

21

Submitting to God's Purposes

*And we know that God causes all things to work together
for good to those who love God, to those who are called
according to His purpose. For whom He foreknew, He also
predestined to become conformed to the image of His Son,
that He might be the first-born among many brethren. . . .*

Romans 8:28-29

———⟡———

How easy it is to become impatient with God's ways. Rather than yield, too often we tend to fight the process God uses to enable us to grow in faith.

The story of Joseph (see Genesis chapters 37, 39-50) is a clear illustration of the truth Paul proclaims in Romans 8:28-29. Over and over again in Joseph's life, we witness a submissive response to God's purposes.

When Joseph's brothers sold him into slavery, we might expect that he would have withdrawn into the pain and hurt of this devastating rejection by his family. Instead, he excelled in everything he did while he was owned by Pharaoh's official, Potiphar. It's as if Joseph said to himself, "Well, I don't like being a slave, but since I am — I'm going to be the best slave Potiphar ever had!" Potiphar was so impressed that he put Joseph in charge of his entire estate.

Then Joseph was falsely accused of assault by Potiphar's wife. Potiphar believed his wife's lie and threw his loyal servant into jail. We would understand if Joseph resented such injustice and spent his days plotting revenge. Yet he earned the unconditional trust of the warden. It's as if he decided, "I don't want to be in prison, but since I am — I'm going to be the best prisoner this jailer has ever seen!" Eventually, as God continued to work all things together for good, Joseph was made a ruler in Egypt.

Many years later, when Joseph's brothers begged him to forgive them for the wrong they had done to him, Joseph answered with a powerful expression of his trust in God's ways: "You meant evil against me," he told them, "but God meant it for good in order to bring about this present result . . ." (Genesis 50:20).

Joseph's life is a powerful example of submitting to the Lord's design for our growth in faith. Because Joseph loved God and trusted His purposes, he knew that God was able to work all things together for good. And our God can do the same for us. When we surrender ourselves to whatever process God chooses to make us more like Him, we can abide in Christ in any circumstances for the glory of God.

View your present afflictions in this light, as chastisements of love. . . . Think with yourself, "It is thus that God is making me more conformable to his own Son; it is thus that he is training me up for complete glory. Thus he kills my corruptions; thus he strengthens my graces; thus he is wisely contriving to bring me nearer to himself, and to ripen me for the honours of his heavenly kingdom."

PHILIP DODDRIDGE

REFLECT: How can I be more patient with the process of becoming like Christ?

Lord, I desire to trust Your purposes in my life. Help me to view my present circumstances not as hindrances, but as opportunities to grow and to reflect Your character. May I willingly submit to the process You have chosen to make me like Your precious Son. AMEN.

22

Taking a Stand

But there were standing by the cross of Jesus
His mother, and His mother's sister,
Mary the wife of Clopas, and Mary Magdalene.

John 19:25

Our youngest son recently graduated from college. The ceremony was especially moving because of a tradition the students observed. As the graduates walked across the stage to receive their diplomas, the friends with whom they had studied, eaten, conversed, played, and shared their lives all stood up. They were silently saying, "This is my friend."

This show of support and friendship touched me deeply. I began to think about how important it is to *stand up for* and *stand by* our friends. What a powerful testimony this demonstration was to all of us who were watching.

Then I thought, *What if Jesus' name were called—who would stand? Who would say, "This is my Friend: I will stand because we have such a relationship that whenever His name is mentioned, I want to be identified with Him"?*

Of course it's easy to stand for Jesus in a friendly crowd. But who will stand for Him when His name is disparaged or taken in vain? Who will stand when standing might mean persecution or ridicule?

When I am with friends who do not know Christ, it is hard for me to identify myself with the Lord. I find it easier just to keep quiet. I am challenged by the women at the cross. They were there to stand with Jesus, saying silently to everyone, "We love Him so much that we will suffer with Him. He is our Friend." May this also be our testimony of love.

Beneath the cross of Jesus
I gladly take my stand:
The shadow of a mighty rock
Within a weary land,
A home within the wilderness,
A rest upon the way,
From the burning of the noon-tide heat
And the burden of the day.

ELIZABETH C. CLEPHANE

REFLECT: Where has God placed me to take a stand for Jesus?

Lord, I choose to take the shadow of Your cross as my abiding place. May my abiding be so deep that standing up for You will never have to be a conscious choice against the prompting of my own desires. AMEN.

23

Watching with Jesus

*Then Jesus came with them to a place called Gethsemane,
and said to His disciples, "Sit here while I go over there
and pray." And He took with Him Peter and the two
sons of Zebedee, and began to be grieved and distressed.
Then He said to them, "My soul is deeply grieved, to the
point of death; remain here and keep watch with Me."*

Matthew 26:36-38

I remember, as a new Christian, reading a short publication entitled *My Heart, Christ's Home* by Robert Boyd
Munger. The booklet sets up an imaginative scenario in
which a man invites Christ to make Himself at home in
his heart.

Although the author promises to meet the Lord
daily in the drawing room of his heart, after a while he
begins to neglect their times together. "One day as I
passed the drawing room," he writes, "the door was ajar.
Looking in I saw a fire in the fireplace and the Lord sitting there. I said, 'Blessed Master, forgive me. Have you
been here all these mornings?' 'Yes,' He said, 'I told you
I would be here every morning to meet with you. . . . The
trouble with you is this: You have been thinking of the
quiet time, of the Bible study and prayer time, as a factor
in your own spiritual progress, but you have forgotten
that this hour means something to Me also. Remember,

I love you. I have redeemed you at great cost. I desire your fellowship.'"

When Jesus entered the darkness of Gethsemane, He was in deep sorrow. In His anguish, He yearned for Peter, James, and John to "watch" with Him. This word means "keep alert, be on guard, pay attention, be vigilant." But instead of supporting Jesus in the hour of His excruciating need, His friends fell asleep — not once, but three times.

"How small a thing it was that he expected from them — only to *watch with him*," Matthew Henry commented. "If he had bid them do some great thing, had bid them be in an agony with him, or die with him, they thought they could have done it; and yet they could not do it . . ."

We tend to view our times with the Lord strictly for our benefit. How our perspective changes when we realize that the Lord Himself longs for our companionship. He waits for us to meet with Him in the inner chamber of our hearts. Let us not keep Him waiting there alone.

———

Again the loneliness of our Lord comes to me more and more.
How few of us are concerned about satisfying His heart.
How I hear Him saying, I thirst, Give me to drink.
May my Lord never let me grow cold in my longing to be a
cup in His hand for the quenching of His own royal thirst.

OSWALD CHAMBERS

———

REFLECT: Where can I look today for an opportunity to "keep watch" with Jesus?

Lord, how easily I am distracted from being with You. Thank You for the reminder that You want to be with me. You delight in my fellowship. You long for me to know You. Hold me faithful to keep watch with You. AMEN.

24

Be on the Alert

*Therefore, be on the alert — for you do not know when
the master of the house is coming, whether in the evening,
at midnight, at cockcrowing, or in the morning —
lest he come suddenly and find you asleep.
And what I say to you I say to all, "Be on the alert!"*

Mark 13:35-37

───────※───────

How will you respond to the Master's return?
I fear that some of my responses might be . . .

"Oh Lord, You're early! Just tomorrow I was going to begin a new plan of reading the Scriptures and set aside special time for prayer."

"You've come just when I was about to read this book that has challenged so many to a deeper commitment."

"Oh Lord, I haven't spent enough time with my family — it's just so hard to get out from under this schedule I've been on."

"Lord, I haven't served You the way I've been intending. If only I'd had more time!"

I remember reading a *Peanuts* cartoon by Charles Schulz, in which Marcie gives her teacher some flowers. Not to be outdone, Peppermint Patty says to the teacher, "I thought about doing the same thing, Ma'am, but I never got around to it. . . . Could you use a vase full of good intentions?"

Few individuals reach the end of their life wishing they had spent more time at the office. Rather, most people tend to regret that they did not spend more time on eternal concerns — the things of God and their relationships with loved ones. Someday, we will give account for how we have lived our lives. We will answer for the choices we have made. Let us not be surprised with dismay and regret, but ready and eager for His coming.

[Watch] for his coming, that it may not at any time be a surprise to you, and pray for that grace which is necessary to qualify you for it, for ye know not when the time is; *and you are concerned to be ready for that* every day, *which may come* any day.

MATTHEW HENRY

REFLECT: Where do I feel God might be prompting me to put "good intentions" into practice?

Lord, I do not want to be ashamed when I see You. I want to live each day as if it were my last. Teach me to be on the alert for Your coming, and to live in light of that day. AMEN.

25

Guarding Against Distractions

Turn away my eyes from looking at vanity,
And revive me in Thy ways.

Psalm 119:37

On rare occasions I have watched the television program "Lifestyles of the Rich and Famous." After observing the opulence of these jetsetters' multiple homes and hearing all the lush details of their exotic trips, I was often left feeling deprived!

Certainly there is nothing wrong with living amid beautiful surroundings. The problem arises when acquiring material things takes on such importance that it becomes a primary source of meaning for our lives. Then we need to pray along with the psalmist, "Turn away my eyes from beholding vanity [idols and idolatry]" (119:37, AMP).

Vanity is hollowness, emptiness, fruitlessness — the characteristics of the lifeless, man-made idols of wood and stone condemned by the prophets (for example, see Isaiah 37:19). Devoting our lives to accumulating bigger, better, and more ultimately produces emptiness in the midst of much. If our focus is on the material or the temporal, our lives will be fruitless. Anything that we hold on to or treasure more than our relationship with the Lord becomes an idol.

This is indeed a challenge, because material things are so attractive. Many of them appeal quite easily to our pride and ambition. Eve struggled with these desires when she yielded to temptation in the garden. She "saw that the tree was good for food, and that it was a delight to the eyes, and that the tree was desirable to make one wise" (Genesis 3:6).

What are the thoughts, relationships, or activities that continually pull us into a lifestyle of compromise or neglect of the Lord and His Word? The world's ways are plastered across T-shirts and bumper stickers in such slogans as, "He who has the most toys wins." Now more than ever we need to sing with the psalmist, "I have rejoiced in the way of Thy testimonies, as much as in all riches" (119:14).

Turn your eyes upon Jesus;
Look full in His wonderful face,
And the things of earth will grow strangely dim
In the light of His glory and grace.

HELEN LEMMEL

REFLECT: What distractions tend to draw my focus away from the Lord?

Lord, I am not rich or famous by the world's standards, but I am rich in Your love and acceptance of me. You know me intimately, and I am precious in Your sight. Keep my focus clear of empty distractions, of anything that keeps me from You. AMEN.

26

Just Passing Through

[We] are afflicted in every way, but not crushed;
perplexed but not despairing; persecuted, but not forsaken;
struck down, but not destroyed.

2 Corinthians 4:8-9

Our son-in-law, Mark, is a fighter pilot. One time, during a visit, he was able to let me experience what it is like to be a pilot by using the F-15E flight simulator. I sat in a virtual cockpit with video screens all around me recording my speed, altitude, and ability to keep the plane level and on the right course.

I was a couple of minutes into the flight when Mark, who was in the back seat, calmly told me over the earphones, "Oops, you just crashed! Let's get you up and going again."

As I later reflected on this experience I thought, *How like the Christian life!* The evidence indicated that I had crashed, but since it was only a simulation flight I was still alive, able to recover and resume flying. And so it is with us. We may be struck down, but we cannot ultimately be destroyed because we have been born again to eternal life. Our lives are now hidden — concealed, safe, secure — in Christ with God (see Colossians 3:3).

As we remember that this physical life is fleeting — essentially a simulation flight for our life with God to come — we can be freed from anxiety. This world is not our final destination! We are strangers and pilgrims; we are just passing through on our way to our permanent home. This confidence gives us inner peace and rest despite difficult circumstances.

Maintaining an eternal perspective on our lives is necessary to responding to the times of affliction, the times of perplexity, the times of persecution, the times of being struck down. As we affirm yet again that this life is only temporary, we will strengthen our ability to persevere and deepen our longing for heaven. Our flight may be turbulent, but when we finally land we will greatly rejoice for all the ways in which the Lord guided us to our destination.

You shall not toil here long,
nor always be oppressed with griefs.
A time will come when all labor and trouble will cease.
Labor faithfully in My vineyard; I will be thy recompense.
Life everlasting is worth all these conflicts, and greater
than these. Are not all plentiful labors to be endured
for the sake of life eternal?
Lift your face therefore unto heaven;
behold, I and all My saints with Me —
who in this world had great conflicts —
are now comforted, now rejoicing, now secure,
now at rest, and shall remain with me everlastingly
in the kingdom of My Father.

THOMAS À KEMPIS

REFLECT: What is one significant way in which I would like to renew my perspective on eternal things?

———— 🐚 ————

Lord, it's hard to remember that this world is not my home. Give me a renewed perspective on this life; give me a longing for the eternal; give me strength to endure the crashes that I experience here. Thank You that no matter what happens I am not ultimately crushed or destroyed, for my life is secure in You. AMEN.

27

Freedom from Entanglement

*No soldier in active service entangles himself
in the affairs of everyday life, so that he may please
the one who enlisted him as a soldier.*

2 Timothy 2:4

Alone in a Roman prison, nearing the end of his life at the hands of the Emperor Nero, Paul wrote his second letter to his young disciple, Timothy. One of the great concerns on the apostle's heart was to encourage Timothy in lifelong faithfulness as a soldier of Christ.

In this epistle we are privileged to learn many important insights for abiding in Christ. One key to remaining strong in our Christian service is to maintain our focus on the concerns of the Lord — to avoid becoming entangled in "the affairs of everyday life."

To *entangle* means "to twist together so that disengagement is difficult; to complicate, to confuse." Do you ever feel that you are so enmeshed in obligations that disengagement is difficult?

Early in my Christian life, the Lord made it clear to me that I needed to keep my involvements to a minimum so that I could be available for the unexpected He wanted to bring into my life. I've learned over the years that confidence in handling the commitments I make is no guarantee that life will be smooth and unencumbered. When the unplanned intrudes, my life quickly becomes complicated and confused.

This factor of the unexpected has become part of my understanding of what it means to stay free of entanglement. I have learned to make short-term commitments and to be very careful in accepting a responsibility over the phone. I'm still in the process of learning to pray in order to seek the Lord's pleasure before I agree to take on a responsibility.

I know few people who do not struggle with complicated lives. When we allow these complexities to preoccupy us, they draw our focus away from Christ. Instead of focusing on pleasing the One who has called us into His service, our lives become driven by our overinvolvement in the affairs of everyday life.

It is time once again to heed the words of our Lord to Martha. We worry and fuss over so many things, but there's really only one thing needful: to sit at the feet of Jesus. This is what will lead us into a lifetime of faithful service — a life that pleases the One who has enlisted us as His soldier.

If we have given up ourselves to be Christ's soldiers, we must sit loose to this world; and though there is no remedy, but we must employ ourselves in the affairs of this life while we are here, we must not entangle ourselves with those affairs, so as by them to be diverted and drawn aside from our duty to God. . . .

MATTHEW HENRY

REFLECT: Where am I most likely to become entangled in the affairs of everyday life?

Lord, too often I find it hard to say no. I don't want to become so entangled that I'm not available for what You want me to do. I want to be in active service. Grant me a discerning heart in knowing what pleases You. AMEN.

28

Longing for God's Word

My soul is crushed with longing
After Thine ordinances at all times.

Psalm 119:20

───────── ⬛ ─────────

Psalm 119 is the longest psalm in the Bible. We might think that because of the sheer number of its verses (176), along with the technique of repetition in Hebrew poetry, this psalm might be slow going in places. Yet as I have been memorizing portions of this psalm, I have been amazed at how profound each verse is on its own — quantity does not diminish quality. Phrase builds upon phrase as the psalmist beautifully extols the wonders of the Word of God, intimately revealing his deep desire to know and experience God more fully.

The twentieth verse has particularly impressed me with the intensity of feeling the writer has for the Scriptures. His desire is so penetrating that his soul seems "crushed" (*The New International Version* renders it "consumed") with its force.

When Jack and I were newly married, the Air Force sent him to Korea while I lived in Japan for a year. After we returned to West Texas, I became pregnant and developed a craving for Japanese food. Although we were now thousands of miles away, my desire persisted: the smell and taste of sukiyaki rarely left my thoughts! Perhaps each of us — whether male or female, pregnant or not — has experienced a craving or longing that seemed overwhelming.

Oh that our hearts would be so crushed with longing for the Scriptures! Oh that our spirits would yearn to be fed by the Word of God. This desire will keep us consistently sitting at the feet of our Lord, exploring the depths of His Word with hearts that hunger for the delight of meeting Him there.

How few are there even among the servants of God who know anything of the intense feeling of devotion here expressed! O that our cold and stubborn hearts were warmed and subdued by divine grace, that we might be ready to faint by reason of the longing which he has at all times for the judgments of our God. How fitful are our best feelings! If to-day we ascend the mount of communion with God, to-morrow we are in danger of being again entangled with the things of earth. How happy are they whose hearts are at all times filled with longings after fellowship with the great and glorious object of their love!

JOHN MORISON

REFLECT: What are some practical ways through which I can deepen my longing for the Scriptures?

Lord, I have not even begun to be consumed with longing for Your Word. Create in me a hunger for Your ways. May my heart be satisfied with nothing else than Your presence and Your Word. "Whom have I in heaven but Thee? And besides Thee, I desire nothing on earth." AMEN.

29
Thirsting for God Himself

O God, Thou art my God; I shall seek Thee earnestly;
My soul thirsts for Thee, my flesh yearns for Thee,
In a dry and weary land where there is no water.

Psalm 63:1

At Easter one year, our family hiked twelve miles down to the Grand Canyon. The trail was rough and rugged, and there were no pools of water for refreshment. Each of us had to carry our own drinking water. The desert has its own beauty, but it is sparse and dry.

It is the desert wilderness of Judah in which David, an outcast from his own home, sings to the Lord the poignant opening words of Psalm 63. David's son Absalom has rebelled against his father and usurped the throne. Family strife has turned their lives upside down. The arid loneliness of the desert mirrors David's inner condition. His soul is in anguish — parched and dry.

We might expect that the rest of this psalm would be a lament over the frailty of human faithfulness and the pain of betrayal. But amid these devastating circumstances, David throws himself upon the Lord. His thirst expresses his inmost desire for communion with God during this period of human abandonment. Instead of dwelling on his adversity, David dwells on God. "Thus I have beheld Thee in the sanctuary, To see Thy power and Thy glory" (verse 2).

Because David seeks God so earnestly, he is able to turn his thoughts from personal adversity to recalling God's lovingkindness and help in the past. This remembrance is what gives David hope amid uncertain and agonizing circumstances.

During personal crisis, we often cling to the belief that if only our circumstances would change, then we would be able to praise God. But David realizes that God is the only One who can satisfy the deepest need of his soul. This is why he is able to praise the Lord.

May we be challenged by David's response. When we feel that life has overwhelmed us, that we are dwelling in a dry and weary land, may we seek the Lord earnestly and thirst for His refreshment and comfort.

He doth not say my soul thirsteth for water, but my soul thirsteth for thee; nor he doth not say my soul thirsteth for the blood of my enemies, but my soul thirsteth for thee; nor he doth not say my soul thirsteth for deliverance out of this dry and barren wilderness, but my soul thirsteth for thee in a dry and thirsty land, where no water is; nor he doth not say my soul thirsteth for a crown, a kingdom, but my soul thirsteth for thee, my flesh longeth for thee.

THOMAS BROOKS

REFLECT: Where in my life is the "dry and weary land" that makes me most keenly aware of my thirst for the Lord Himself?

Lord, when I feel dry and weary, when life seems overwhelming, remind me that my true need is for You. You alone can satisfy the depths of my soul. "Because Thy lovingkindness is better than life, My lips will praise Thee. So I will bless Thee as long as I live; I will lift up my hands in Thy name" [Psalm 63:3-4]. AMEN.

30

The Courts of the Lord

For a day in Thy courts is better than a thousand outside.
I would rather stand at the threshold of the house of
my God, Than dwell in the tents of wickedness.

Psalm 84:10

The world and its dark ruler beckon us to live in ways that indulge the flesh. The promised satisfactions are endless and the enticements alluring. How tempting it is to settle down, get comfortable, and escape — even fleetingly — to a worldly tent.

Recently, I asked God to show me the inclinations I have that might lead me away from His courts. I was struck by the relevance to my life of Psalm 141:4, which warns against "eating the delicacies" of sin. Although I am seldom tempted to sin blatantly, I am inclined to eat around its edges.

To keep from sampling the delicacies of sin, we must be convinced that even a humble dwelling in the house of the Lord is a thousand times better than any palace the world has to offer. We must desire to mature from drinking the milk of the Word to eating solid food. The writer of Hebrews states, "But solid food is for the mature, who because of practice have their senses trained to discern good and evil" (5:14). Only as we abide in Christ consistently will we be able to discern the subtleties of sin.

I remember hearing this piercing truth: "Either sin will keep you from God's Word, or God's Word will keep you from sin." It is encouraging to know that as we hunger and thirst for righteousness, we will be filled — and able to resist the call of the Enemy. We will affirm, with David, that the fellowship of the Lord is far better than the fellowship of the world: "For the LORD God is a sun and shield; the LORD gives grace and glory; no good thing does He withhold from those who walk uprightly" (Psalm 84:11).

To feel his love, to rejoice in the person of the anointed Savior, to survey the promises and feel the power of the Holy Ghost in applying precious truth to the soul, is a joy which worldlings cannot understand, but which true believers are ravished with. . . . Every man has his choice, and this is ours. God's worst is better than the devil's best. God's doorstep is a happier rest than downy couches within the pavilions of royal sinners, though we might lie there for a lifetime of luxury.

CHARLES SPURGEON

REFLECT: Where am I most often prompted to make a choice between dwelling in the "courts of the Lord" or lingering in the "tents" of the world?

Lord, how lovely is Your dwelling place. It is true that anything the world offers pales in comparison to Your infinite goodness. Only when I take my eyes off You am I tempted by worldly enticements. Increase my longing for the eternal, and let me dwell in Your courts. AMEN.

31

Resting in God

*Come to Me, all who are weary and heavy-laden,
and I will give you rest.*

Matthew 11:28

Someone once asked me the question, "If you had the opportunity to do anything you wanted, what would you choose?" I responded that I would like to take a month and go to a cabin (well-equipped!) to read, rest, pray, and be refreshed by the Lord.

I like to recall Jesus' care for the disciples when their pace was so hectic that they didn't even have time to eat: "Come away by yourselves to a lonely place and rest a while," He said to them (Mark 6:31). I love this passage because it reminds us that Jesus and the disciples lived in the real world just as we do, and it portrays the tender concern Jesus had for His disciples' human needs.

I am challenged by Jesus' own example of getting away. The Scriptures tell us, "But He Himself would often slip away to the wilderness and pray" (Luke 5:16). The Lord needed the rest that only communion with His Father could provide.

This "slipping away" to the wilderness is vital to

preserving the strength and trust we need to go through each day. Coming away to a lonely place by ourselves where we meet the Lord, read His Word, pray, and commune daily with Him is one way of receiving rest.

I also think that the Lord wants us to practice the art of slipping away *often* throughout the day. "Often" can be any time we sense anxiety, anger, or frustration controlling our behavior — or any time we need grace, strength, or wisdom. Slipping away does not require that we cease our activities. We can go to Him in the quietness of our hearts, share our burden, and find rest for our souls.

It is fitting to conclude this series of devotional reflections with our Lord's gracious invitation to *come to Him*. I hope you will be encouraged by the realization that the process of becoming a woman who walks with God begins and ends with God Himself. It is not dependent upon what you do or who you are according to earthly standards. It is first and foremost rooted in abiding in Christ, desiring to spend time with Him more than anything else in the world. May this abiding become your greatest treasure and delight as you walk with God.

[Rest] is the mind at leisure from itself. It is the perfect poise of the soul; the absolute adjustment of the inward man to the stress of all outward things; the preparedness against every emergency; the stability of assured convictions; the eternal calm of an invulnerable faith; the repose of a heart set deep in God.

HENRY DRUMMOND

REFLECT: In what ways can I continue to pursue a deeper experience of the rest that is promised through abiding in Christ?

Lord, as I come to You, I receive rest. As I sit at Your feet and listen to Your words, I receive wisdom. As I abide in You, I receive strength and the ability to bear fruit. As I walk with You, I become more like You. Forever, may I seek Your abiding presence. AMEN.

In the Garden

I come to the garden alone,
While the dew is still on the roses;
And the voice I hear, falling on my ear,
The Son of God discloses.

And He walks with me,
And He talks with me,
And He tells me I am His own;
And the joy we share as we tarry there,
None other has ever known.

C. Austin Miles

Sources

Note: Multiple entries for a particular section are listed in the order of their appearance in the text.

EPIGRAPH (PAGE 5)
A. W. Tozer, *The Pursuit of God* (Camp Hill, Penn.: Christian Publications, 1982), page 20.

1 — THE SECURITY OF ABIDING
Andrew Murray, *Daily Secrets of Christian Living*, compiled by Al Bryant (Minneapolis: Bethany Fellowship, 1978), 4 July.

2 — CHOOSING TO ABIDE
Ken Gire, *Intimate Moments with the Savior* (Grand Rapids: Zondervan/Daybreak, 1989), page 47.

3 — ABIDING IN THE WORD
R. A. Torrey, *How to Pray* (Chicago: Moody Press, 1958), page 59.

4 — BEARING FRUIT
Roger C. Palms, *The Pleasure of His Company* (Wheaton: Tyndale House Publishers, 1983), page 88.

5 — ONE DAY AT A TIME
C. S. Lewis, *Letters to an American Lady* (Grand Rapids: William B. Eerdmans, 1971), page 103.

6 — FLYING FIRST CLASS
Amy Carmichael, *Whispers of His Power* (Old Tappan, N.J.: Fleming H. Revell, 1982), 8 June and 10 June, pages 107 and 108.

7 — "MY" GOD CARES

Matthew Henry, *Commentary on the Whole Bible*, Psalm
XVIII, section I (Iowa Falls: Riverside Book and Bible
House; Christian Booksellers ed.), page 296.

8 — GOD WITH US

Ken Gire, *Intimate Moments with the Savior*, page 7.

9 — FOLLOWING IN HIS PRESENCE

Amy Carmichael, *Edges of His Ways* (Fort Washington,
Penn.: Christian Literature Crusade, 1989), page 139.

10 — THE GRACE OF PATIENCE

Robert Jamieson, A. R. Fausset, and David Brown,
Commentary on the Whole Bible (Grand Rapids: Zondervan
Publishing House, 1979), page 1149.

11 — REST AND WAIT

Jerome, quoted in Charles H. Spurgeon, *The Treasury of
David* (McLean, Vir.: MacDonald Publishing Company,
n.d.), vol. I, part 2, Psalm 37, page 185.

Charles H. Spurgeon, *The Treasury of David*, vol. I, part 1,
Psalm 25, page 393.

12 — RESPONDING TO PAINFUL CIRCUMSTANCES

Robert Jamieson, A. R. Fausset, and David Brown,
Commentary on the Whole Bible, page 1311.

13 — PROTECTION FROM DISCOURAGEMENT

Robert Baylie, from "Sermon before the House of
Commons, 1643," quoted in Spurgeon, *The Treasury of
David*, vol. I, part 2, Psalm 37, page 183.

14 — THE POWER OF PERSEVERANCE

William Gurnall, *The Christian in Complete Armour*, abridged
by Ruthanne Garlock, et al. (Carlisle, Penn.: Banner of
Truth Trust, 1989), vol. I, page 33.

15 — JOY IN TRIALS

William Gurnall, *The Christian in Complete Armour*, page 134.

16 — UNCONDITIONAL TRUST
From the hymn "All the Way My Savior Leads Me," lyrics
by Fanny J. Crosby, in *Hymns for the Family of God*
(Nashville: Paragon Associates, 1976), no. 598.

17 — SUFFERING AND GLORY
A. W. Tozer, *The Pursuit of God*, page 59.

18 — THE FAITHFULNESS OF GOD
Charles H. Spurgeon, *The Treasury of David*, vol. II, part 1,
Psalm 62, page 50.

19 — STRENGTH FOR THE WEARY
Matthew Henry, *Commentary on the Whole Bible*, Isaiah
XLI:27-31, section II.2.(I), page 219.

20 — THE POTTER AND THE CLAY
Hannah Whitall Smith, *The Christian's Secret of a Happy Life*
(Westwood, N.J.: Fleming H. Revell, 1952), page 211.

21 — SUBMITTING TO GOD'S PURPOSES
Philip Doddridge, quoted in *Giant Steps: Daily Devotions from
Spiritual Giants of the Past,* edited by Warren W. Wiersbe
(Grand Rapids: Baker Book House, 1981), page 48.

22 — TAKING A STAND
From the hymn "Beneath the Cross of Jesus," lyrics by
Elizabeth C. Clephane, in *Hymns for the Family of God,*
no. 253.

23 — WATCHING WITH JESUS
Robert Boyd Munger, *My Heart Christ's Home* (Downers
Grove: InterVarsity Press, 1954), pages 11-12.

Matthew Henry, *Commentary on the Whole Bible*, Matthew
XXVI, section VI.2.(2).[3], page 398.

Oswald Chambers, in *Oswald Chambers: Abandoned to God,* by
David McCasland (Nashville: Thomas Nelson/
Discovery House Publishers, 1993), page 167.

24 — BE ON THE ALERT
Matthew Henry, *Commentary on the Whole Bible*, Mark XIV,
section III, page 545.

25 — GUARDING AGAINST DISTRACTIONS
From the hymn "Turn Your Eyes upon Jesus," lyrics and
music by Helen H. Lemmel, in *Hymns for the Family of
God*, no. 621.

26 — JUST PASSING THROUGH
Thomas à Kempis, quoted in *Closer Walk* (Atlanta: Walk
Thru the Bible, 1987), 20/21 August.

27 — FREEDOM FROM ENTANGLEMENT
Matthew Henry, *Commentary on the Whole Bible*, 2 Timothy
II, section III, page 838.

28 — LONGING FOR GOD'S WORD
John Morison, quoted in Spurgeon, *The Treasury of David*,
vol III, part I, Psalm 119:20, page 183.

29 — THIRSTING FOR GOD HIMSELF
Thomas Brooks, quoted in Spurgeon, *The Treasury of David*,
vol II, part I, Psalm 63:1, page 69.

30 — THE COURTS OF THE LORD
Charles H. Spurgeon, *The Treasury of David*, vol II, part I,
Psalm 84:10, page 435.

31 — RESTING IN GOD
Henry Drummond, quoted in *Giant Steps*, page 246.

EPIGRAPH (PAGE 89)
From the hymn "In the Garden," lyrics and music by C.
Austin Miles, in *Hymns for the Family of God*, no. 588.

Author

CYNTHIA HALL HEALD is a native Texan. She and her husband, Jack, a veterinarian by profession, are on full-time staff with The Navigators in Tucson, Arizona. They have four children: Melinda, Daryl, Shelly, and Michael.

Cynthia graduated from the University of Texas with a B.A. in English. She speaks frequently to church women's groups and at seminars and retreats.

Cynthia is also the author of the NavPress Bible studies *Becoming a Woman of Excellence; Becoming a Woman of Freedom; Intimacy with God: Pursuing a Deeper Experience of God Through the Psalms;* and *Loving Your Husband: Building an Intimate Marriage in a Fallen World* (companion study to *Loving Your Wife: Building an Intimate Marriage in a Fallen World* by Jack and Cynthia Heald).

Other Motivating Titles from Cynthia Heald.

Becoming a Woman of Excellence
978-1-57683-832-7

Becoming a Woman of Freedom
978-1-57683-829-7

Becoming a Woman of Purpose
978-1-57683-831-0

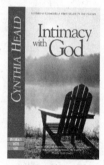

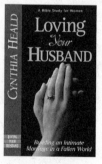

Intimacy with God
978-0-89109-140-0

Loving Your Husband
978-0-89109-544-6

To order copies, call NavPress at 1-800-366-7788
or log on to www.navpress.com.

Discipleship Inside Out™